CONFLICTS AND INDEPENDENCE

BY JIM OLLHOFF

VISIT US AT
WWW.ABDOPUBLISHING.COM

Published by ABDO Publishing Company, 8000 West 78th Street, Suite 310, Edina, MN 55439. Copyright ©2012 by Abdo Consulting Group, Inc. International copyrights reserved in all countries. No part of this book may be reproduced in any form without written permission from the publisher. ABDO & Daughters™ is a trademark and logo of ABDO Publishing Company.

Printed in the United States of America, North Mankato, Minnesota.
052011
092011

 PRINTED ON RECYCLED PAPER

Editor: John Hamilton
Graphic Design: Sue Hamilton
Cover Design: Neil Klinepier
Cover Photo: Granger Collection
Interior Photos and Illustrations: AP-pgs 6, 7, 18, 19, 24 & 28; Corbis-pg 25; Getty Images-pgs 4, 5, 20 & 21; Granger Collection-pgs 8-17, 22 & 23; iStockphoto-pg 18 (inset), Library of Congress-pgs 26, 27 & 29.

Library of Congress Cataloging-in-Publication Data

Ollhoff, Jim, 1959-
  Conflicts and independence / Jim Ollhoff.
    p. cm. -- (Hispanic American history)
  Includes index.
  ISBN 978-1-61783-054-9
  1. Latin America--History--Juvenile literature. 2. Hispanic Americans--History--Juvenile literature. I. Title.
  F1410.O47 2012
  980--dc23
                    2011017711

CONTENTS

LIBERATION IN LATIN AMERICA

Beginning in the late 1400s and early 1500s, Spain started many colonies in the New World. These areas are part of what today we call Latin America. They included many parts of South and Central America, including Mexico. The Spanish also started colonies in today's states of Florida, Texas, New Mexico, Arizona, and California.

Other countries also started colonies. The British claimed much of the eastern part of today's United States. The French claimed the Mississippi River and all lands connected to it. The European powers jostled for control of their colonies. Wars often broke out.

The colonies began to revolt against the European powers. The relationship between Spain and its Latin American colonies grew worse and worse. In the early 1800s, Spain lost almost all of its colonies in the New World.

As the United States grew to become a world power, it entered the conflicts, too. For the Latin American colonists, the 1800s were a time of fighting for freedom.

During a hurricane in 1565, Spanish soldiers attacked Fort Caroline, France's only established settlement in Florida.

5

SPAIN AND THE LATIN AMERICAN COLONIES

By the late 1700s and early 1800s, many Latin Americans were angry at Spain. They felt that the Spanish king was mistreating them. Latin American countries weren't allowed to choose their own governors or other administrators. The King of Spain appointed all the important administrative positions—and he only appointed Europeans to rule in Latin America. He refused to let local-born people rule.

Latin American colonies usually were not allowed to trade with other countries. They couldn't even trade with a country right next to them. They could only trade with Spain. This ensured a big market for Spanish goods. The arrangement was good for Spain, but not so good for the Latin American colonies. The Spanish didn't pay very well for Latin American products, which made the Latin Americans angry.

Under Spanish rule, Latin American colonists were only allowed to trade with Spain.

Another law said that Latin Americans could never criticize Spain, the Spanish administrators, or any of their decisions. Latin Americans were not allowed to have free speech. If people spoke out against a Spanish governor or an unfair law, they could be thrown in jail.

All these things made Latin Americans angry at Spain, and they began to think that they should rule themselves.

Spain forced the Latin American colonies to pay heavy taxes, too. The Spanish claimed the taxes were important because Spain's military protected the colonies. However, in 1806, the British attacked Argentina, and Spain did not do a good job protecting its colonists. It was the Argentineans, not the Spanish, who fought and defeated the British. This spurred Latin American colonies to think that they might win a war of independence. After all, the colonists in the United States had just won a war of independence against the British.

Spain was in trouble. Its economy was in shambles because it had been fighting other European countries for many years. In 1808, French Emperor Napoléon Bonaparte marched his troops into Spain. Napoléon put his brother on the Spanish throne. This made the colonies think Spain was weak, which made them bolder about declaring their independence.

In the early 1800s, Latin American colonists began to believe they could win a war of independence from Spain.

THE REVOLUTIONS BEGIN

When the French invaded Spain in 1808, several Central American countries used it as an opportunity to declare their independence. Since Spain was busy with its own internal problems, it never sent any troops to stop the revolution in Central America. Spain officially granted the colonies their independence in 1821.

Venezuela declared its independence from Spain in 1811, but struggled to maintain it. Finally, 10 years later, under the leadership of Simón Bolívar, Venezuela won its independence from Spain.

Venezuelan revolutionary Francisco de Miranda (standing with sword) watches the signing of the Act of Independence in Venezuela on July 5, 1811.

Simón Bolívar (1783–1830)

Born in Venezuela, Simón Bolívar is sometimes called the "George Washington of South America." As a young man in 1798, Bolívar was sent to Europe to continue his education. He saw firsthand the problems in Europe. When he returned to Venezuela in 1807, he vowed not to rest until South America was free.

Bolívar gathered followers and led the independence movement against Spain. He helped liberate many South American countries, including Venezuela, Colombia, Peru, Ecuador, Panama, and Bolivia. Bolivia is named in his honor. Simón Bolívar is often called *El Libertador,* which means "The Liberator."

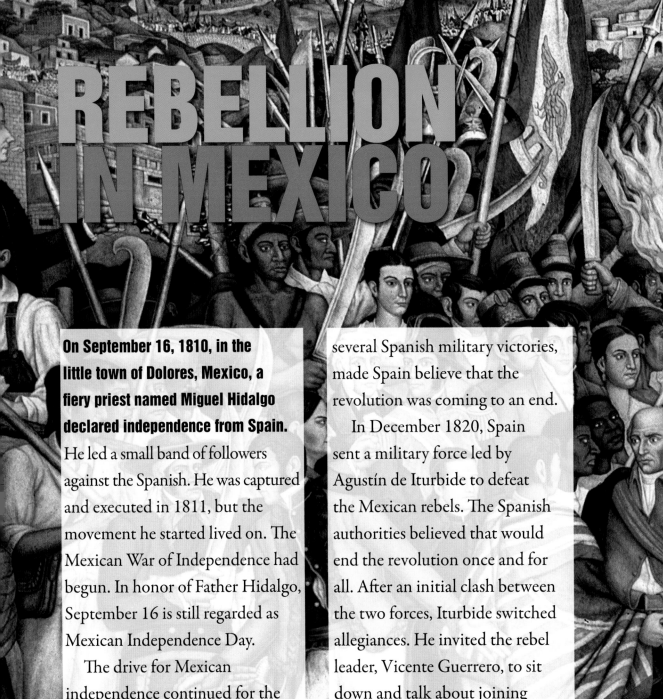

REBELLION IN MEXICO

On September 16, 1810, in the little town of Dolores, Mexico, a fiery priest named Miguel Hidalgo declared independence from Spain. He led a small band of followers against the Spanish. He was captured and executed in 1811, but the movement he started lived on. The Mexican War of Independence had begun. In honor of Father Hidalgo, September 16 is still regarded as Mexican Independence Day.

The drive for Mexican independence continued for the next 10 years. Battles between Spanish authorities and Mexican fighters continued in a variety of places around Mexico. Infighting between Mexican groups, plus several Spanish military victories, made Spain believe that the revolution was coming to an end.

In December 1820, Spain sent a military force led by Agustín de Iturbide to defeat the Mexican rebels. The Spanish authorities believed that would end the revolution once and for all. After an initial clash between the two forces, Iturbide switched allegiances. He invited the rebel leader, Vicente Guerrero, to sit down and talk about joining forces for Mexican independence. They created a plan that united all the Mexican groups. Independence was finally won in 1821.

Father Hidalgo declares independence from Spain in 1810.

13

UNITED STATES AND MANIFEST DESTINY

In the early 1800s, the world's superpowers were all jockeying for control of the New World. Spain was trying to regain influence in Latin America. Great Britain wanted to trade with Latin America without Spanish interference. Great Britain and Spain were trying to keep the French from taking over Europe. Russia was laying claim to huge sections of northwest North America.

The new power on the world's stage was the United States. The young nation had defeated Great Britain in the Revolutionary War (1775–1783) and battled to a draw in the War of 1812 (1812–1815). The United States was suspicious of the European powers and their intentions in Latin America. The United States was afraid of the Europeans keeping a foothold in the New World, from which they might launch attacks.

In 1823, James Monroe, the fifth president of the United States, made a proclamation. He said that the European powers should stay out of Latin America for good, and that the Latin Americans should govern themselves. This proclamation became known as the Monroe Doctrine. At that time, the United States lacked the military might to back up the Monroe Doctrine. However, many Latin Americans were delighted, and rallied behind the United States.

In 1823, U.S. President James Monroe proclaimed that Latin Americans should govern themselves. This became known as the Monroe Doctrine.

As time wore on, people in the United States began to move farther west, and an idea called "Manifest Destiny" began to take hold. Manifest Destiny was the idea that people in the United States had a divine right to own all the land from the Atlantic to the Pacific Ocean. They believed that the land was theirs, and that they had the right to displace the Native Americans and take the land.

People in the United States looked at the large land holdings of Mexico and began to desire that land, too. The United States began to believe that Florida, Texas, Arizona, New Mexico, and California should be possessions of the United States. Some people even thought the United States should simply take the land, rather than buy it or negotiate for it.

People in the United States believed they had the divine right to settle all the land from one side of the country to the other. This became known as Manifest Destiny.

WESTWARD EXPANSION

In the late 1600s and early 1700s, the French laid claim to present-day Louisiana and built forts there. Spain was afraid the French would use Louisiana as a base from which to attack Mexico City. So, Spain tried to start a number of missions and forts in eastern Texas. San Antonio was one of the cities that sprung up at this time.

As time went on, different groups argued about who owned Texas. The French sold a huge section of land to the United States in 1803 called the Louisiana Purchase. Many in the United States thought Texas should be a part of that. The Mexicans believed they owned the land, since Spain had owned it before. The Native American nations, who had lived there for hundreds of years, thought they owned their land and aggressively defended it.

LOUISIANA PURCHASE

Many people thought Texas should have been a part of the Louisiana Purchase.

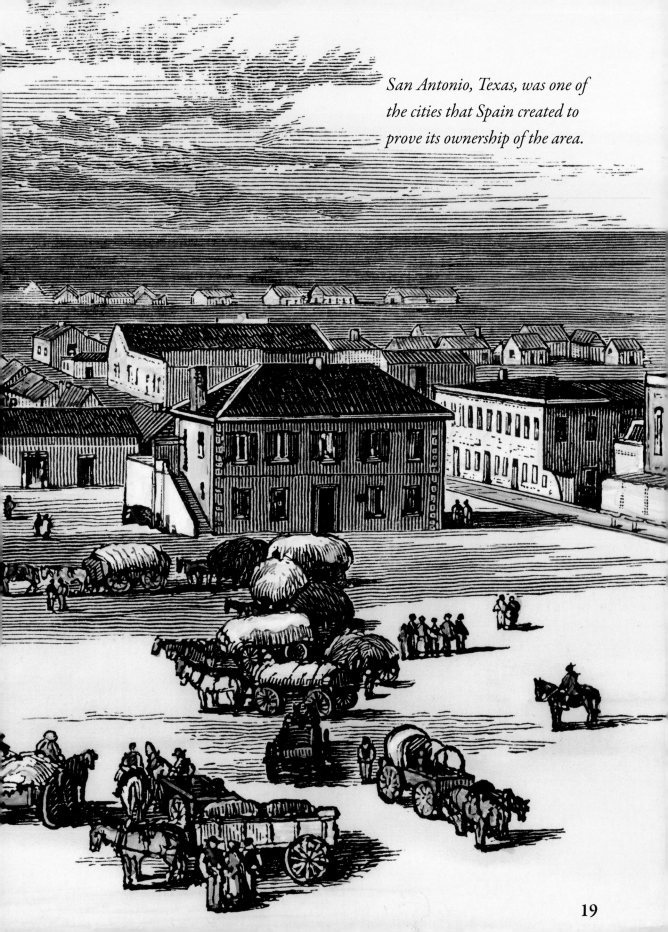

San Antonio, Texas, was one of the cities that Spain created to prove its ownership of the area.

19

After declaring independence from Spain, Mexico did not have the money or resources to send an army to Texas to defend it from Native American attacks. So, Mexico relaxed its immigration policies, thinking more people from Europe and the United States would move to Texas and would defend the countryside from Native American raids.

The new residents of Texas didn't like many of the Mexican laws. They began to talk about separating from Mexico and forming an independent republic. In 1836, the residents of Texas declared that they were independent of Mexico.

Frontiersman Davy Crockett (above) helps defend the Alamo against Mexican forces.

The Mexican dictator Antonio López de Santa Anna led an army to stop the rebellion. One of the most famous battles took place in 1836 at the Alamo, a fort located in modern-day San Antonio, Texas.

During the battle, 257 Texans were killed by a much larger Mexican army. However, the battle inflamed the passions of other Texas residents, and the drive for independence continued. The citizens of Texas wanted to become part of the United States. In 1845, Congress approved Texas's entry into the union of states.

Texas joined the United States in 1845.

THE MEXICAN-AMERICAN WAR

American General Winfield Scott
and his army enter Mexico City
on September 17, 1847.

Mexico refused to recognize Texas's independence. Mexico had told the United States that if Texas became a state, it could mean war. Mexican and United States troops began patrolling the disputed border. In April 1846, a small United States military patrol was attacked by a much larger Mexican force. Inflaming the passions of both sides, negotiations failed as the two countries headed for war.

The Mexican government was troubled with infighting and bickering. Most of their important government positions had changed hands a number of times. In order to have enough soldiers, generals conscripted farmers and merchants and forced them to fight. Because of all this, the Mexican desertion rate was high, and communication between government positions was poor. The United States military won many of the battles, and occupied Mexico City by the fall of 1847. The United States won the war, and took ownership of Texas, California, and most of Arizona and New Mexico.

CALIFORNIA

A California vaquero, or cowboy, rides to lasso a steer.

In the late 1700s, Spanish missionaries began to settle in California. A string of missions stretched up the coast of California. Soon, Hispanic ranchers began moving in and raising cattle. After Mexico won independence in 1821, California became a sparsely populated northern province of Mexico.

Soon, more and more people began filtering into California. Traders, ranchers, and trappers began arriving from the East. In 1846, Californians declared their independence from Mexico, but it was a short independence. The Mexican-American War had begun, and the United States military arrived to occupy California.

In 1848, gold was discovered in California. Hearing exaggerated reports that gold was just lying on the ground, people from all over the world rushed to California. In 1848, the population of California was about 15,000. Six years later, the population had mushroomed to 300,000. In 1850, California became the 31st state of the union.

A prospector pans for gold in California in the 1800s.

THE SPANISH-AMERICAN WAR

People on the Caribbean island of Cuba had been talking about declaring independence for decades. Spain did not want Cuba to be independent, since Cuba was important to Spain's economy. Spanish soldiers in Cuba were keeping an uneasy peace. The United States did not want Spanish influence in Cuba, but continued negotiating. In 1898, a riot broke out in Cuba, and the United States sent in a battleship, the USS *Maine*, to protect American citizens. It exploded in Cuban waters, killing 266 Americans.

The USS Maine *sails into Havana, Cuba, three weeks before it explodes.*

Most people in the United States assumed that it had been destroyed by an underwater Spanish mine, and wanted swift punishment for Spain. Even today, the explosion of the *Maine* remains a mystery. Some experts say the ship accidentally exploded, and others say it was a victim of a naval mine.

The United States and Spain went to war in 1898. However, Spain was very weak from its constant fighting in Europe and the New World. It surrendered after only a few months of war. In less than 100 years, Spain had lost virtually all of its New World colonies. The Spanish Empire had come to an end.

Cuban soldiers stand with the newly independent country's flag.

LOOKING TO THE FUTURE

The 1800s were marked by terrible struggle. Fighting, conflicts, and wars were happening almost constantly. Central and South American countries rebelled from Spain. Countries split up and recombined. Dictators rose and fell. It was a bloody century.

But as the 1900s began, Hispanic Americans were faced with new challenges and opportunities. Hispanic Americans found themselves in many different countries where they could build a future for themselves and their children.

Hispanic people dancing the fandango.

Admiral David Glasgow Farragut (1801–1870)

David Glasgow Farragut was a Hispanic admiral during the American Civil War (1861–1865). His father came to the United States from Spain to help fight in the American Revolution. David Farragut grew up in Tennessee, and joined the Navy at an early age.

As a navy commander, he won several victories for Union forces in the Civil War. In 1864, at the Battle of Mobile Bay, a number of ships charged through the bay, and one was struck by a naval mine. (In those days, mines were called torpedoes.) The ships began to pull back. Farragut called out, "What's the trouble?" The answer came back, "Torpedoes!" Farragut's exact response is unclear, but most people remember the now-famous words, "Damn the torpedoes, full speed ahead!"

GLOSSARY

CROCKETT, DAVY

A frontiersman, trapper, politician, and soldier, Davy Crockett (1786-1836) was sometimes called "King of the Wild Frontier." Although he lived much of his life in Tennessee, he died in Texas at the Battle of the Alamo.

INDEPENDENCE

When a country declares that it is no longer governed by the country that founded or controls it.

LATIN AMERICA

The New World possessions of Spain, including Mexico, Central America, and much of South America and the Caribbean islands.

LOUISIANA PURCHASE

A large area of land in North America purchased from France in 1803. The purchase included much land from the Mississippi River to the Rocky Mountains and from the Gulf of Mexico to the Canadian border.

MANIFEST DESTINY

An idea held by many people in the United States in the 1800s that the country should occupy all the land between the Atlantic Ocean and the Pacific Ocean.

MINE

An underwater bomb that explodes when a ship touches it. During the Civil War, they were called torpedoes.

MIRANDA, FRANCISCO DE

A Venezuelan revolutionary, Miranda (1750-1816) fought for the independence of Spanish American colonies in the New World. Although his dreams of Spanish American freedom did not come true during his lifetime, he paved the way for the successful revolution of much of South America from Spanish rule.

MONROE DOCTRINE

An 1823 proclamation by James Monroe, the fifth president of the United States, that the European powers should stay out of Latin America for good, and that the Latin Americans should govern themselves.

PROCLAMATION

A formal public statement. In 1823, United States President James Monroe proclaimed that European powers should stay out of Latin America for good, and that the Latin Americans should govern themselves. This proclamation became known as the Monroe Doctrine.

REVOLUTIONARY WAR

The war fought between the American colonies and Great Britain from 1775-1783. It is also known as the War of Independence, or the American Revolution. America won its independence in the war.

SUPERPOWERS

A few extremely powerful nations with strong military forces.

INDEX